MONEY *Love* WORKSHOP

MEADOW DEVOR
MONEY COACH

Also by Meadow DeVor

Money Love, A Guide to Changing the Way You Think About Money

The Tao of Rowdy

The Tao of Rowdy Workbook

(c) 2012 by Meadow DeVor

All rights reserved.
This book or parts thereof may not be produced in any form without the author's permission.

ISBN-13: 978-1494219161
ISBN-10: 1494219166

Printed in the United States of America

First Printing 2013

MONEY *Love* WORKSHOP

MEADOW DEVOR
MONEY COACH

Copyright 2013 by Meadow DeVor.
All Rights Reserved

Week 1

Preparing for the Truth

Coaching Notes

Date

Money Love Workshop

Day 1

What does 'telling the truth about your finances' mean to you?

_____

_____

_____

_____

_____

_____

Week 1

Money Love Workshop

Day 2

Is telling the truth about your finances important to you? Why or why not?

_____

_____

_____

_____

_____

Week 1

Money Love Workshop

Day 3

What are you afraid to know or find out in this process? What great news would you love to find out?

_____
_____
_____
_____
_____
_____

Week 1

Day 4

Do you spend money that you do not have? (In other words, do you buy things on credit, use a credit card, or take out loans?) Why or why not?

_____
_____
_____
_____
_____

Week 1

Money Love Workshop

Day 5

What do you think the state of your finances means about you as a person?

_____

_____

_____

_____

_____

Week 1

Money Love Workshop

Day 6

What feelings do you experience when you think about uncovering the truth?

_____

_____

_____

_____

_____

_____

Week 1

Money Love Workshop

How have you justified avoiding the truth in the past? What beliefs have justified avoiding the truth?

_____
_____
_____
_____
_____

Week 1

Week 2

Opening Your Eyes

Coaching Notes

Date

Money Love Workshop

Day 1

List and total all of your "**Money Makers**". These are the things that you can sell for more than you paid for them. (Savings accounts, IRA/SEP/401k, investments without debt, income properties.)

Name/Description	Cash Value
_____	_____
_____	_____
_____	_____
_____	_____
_____	_____
_____	_____

What thoughts do you have regarding your Money Makers?

_____
_____
_____
_____
_____
_____

Week 2

Money Love Workshop

List and total all of your **"Money Takers"**. These are the thing that you can sell for less than you paid. (TV, stereo, computers, tech stuff, furniture, gear, toys, motorcycle/car/RV/boat with no debt, musical instruments, clothing, jewelry, equipment, etc.)

Name/Description	Actual Street Value (Craigslist price)
_____	_____
_____	_____
_____	_____
_____	_____
_____	_____

What thoughts do you have regarding your Money Takers?

_____
_____
_____
_____
_____

Week 2

Money Love Workshop

Day 3

List and total all of your "**Money Breakers**". These are the things that costs you more than you paid. (All credit cards, retail cards, lines of credit, student loans, property loans, mortgages, car loans, business loans, medical/dental/orthodontic loans.)

Name/Description   Pay-off Amount

_____   _____
_____   _____
_____   _____
_____   _____
_____   _____
_____   _____
_____   _____

What thoughts do you have regarding your Money Takers?

_____
_____
_____
_____
_____

Week 2

Money Love Workshop

Day 4

List all the other "**Stuff**". These are the things that you can't really sell, this stuff doesn't retain its value. Kitchen cupboards stuff. Pantry stuff. Refrigerator stuff. Cleaning stuff. Bathroom drawers and cabinets stuff. Garage stuff. Storage stuff. Shelf stuff. Holiday stuff. Technical stuff. Office supply stuff. Guest room stuff. Kids stuff. Linen stuff. Jewelry stuff. Clothing stuff. Make up stuff.

_____   _____
_____   _____
_____   _____
_____   _____
_____   _____

What thoughts do you have regarding your Stuff?

_____
_____
_____
_____

Week 2

Money Love Workshop

Day 5

Figure out your Net Worth.

$Money Makers + $Money Takers + $Stuff - $Money Breakers = Net Worth

$_____ + $_____ + $_____ – $_____ = _____

What thoughts do you have regarding your Net Worth?

_____
_____
_____
_____
_____

Week 2

Money Love Workshop

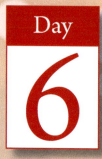
Day 6

What feelings come up for when you look at your Net Worth?
Is it what you were expecting?
Why or why not?

_____

_____

_____

_____

_____

Week 2

Money Love Workshop

Day 7

This process is about discovering the Truth and becoming connected to ourselves and our relationship with money. When you look at the purchases that you have made (and/or continue to make) do they represent the truth for you? Is your house the truth? Is your car the truth? Is your wardrobe the truth? etc. Why or why not?

_____
_____
_____
_____
_____

Week 2

Week 3

The Truth About How You Spend

Coaching Notes

Date

Money Love Workshop

Day 1

On the **Abundance Scale** (-10 being the most scarce, 0 being neutral, and +10 being the most abundant), where do you fall on the Abundance Scale today? Why?

_____

_____

_____

_____

_____

Week 3

Money Love Workshop

Day 2

Neutral Spending is money spent from the neutral zone on the Abundance Scale (-1 to +1). It is an action that is created by neutral feelings and thoughts. What are some examples of Neutral Spending in your current life? What makes these "Neutral Spends"?

_____
_____
_____
_____
_____
_____

Week 3

Day 3

Abundant Spending is money spent from the abundant zone on the Abundance Scale (+2 to +10). This is money spent from an empowered, passionate, appreciative, enthusiastic, optimistic, happy, loving, or grateful place. What are some examples of Abundant Spending in your current life? What makes these "Abundant Spends"?

_____

_____

_____

_____

_____

Week 3

Money Love Workshop

Day 4

Scarcity Spending is money spent from the scarcity zone on the Abundance Scale (-2 to -10). It is an action that is created by scarce/negative feelings and thoughts. What are examples of Scarcity Spending in your current life? What makes these "Scarce Spends"?

_____

_____

_____

_____

_____

Week 3

Money Love Workshop

Day 5

Avoidance Spending is money spent unconsciously in order to not experience scarce/negative feelings and thoughts. Avoidance Spending is money spent in the scarcity zone on the Abundance Scale, even though you do not recognize the feeling at the time. This is an action taken to NOT FEEL something. This is an action usually taken to distract yourself from the truth. It is typically money spent in order to avoid feeling broke, stuck, punished, left out. Avoidance Spending can also be money that you are unconsciously spending because you aren't dealing with your finances (extras like un-used gym memberships, extra cell phone minutes, unused automatic payments, overdraft fees, etc.) What are examples of Avoidance Spending in your current life? What makes these "Avoidance Spends"?

_____

_____

_____

_____

_____

Week 3

Money Love Workshop

Day 6

Is is ever OK to buy something you can't afford (go into debt) in order to feel better?
Why or why not?

_____
_____
_____
_____
_____
_____

Week 3

Is it possible to Abundance Spend or Neutral Spend if you are feeling crappy, angry or frustrated (even if it's just directed toward the store clerk)? Why or why not?

_____

_____

_____

_____

_____

Week 3

Week 4

The Truth About How You Earn:

Coaching Notes

Date:

Money Love Workshop

Day 1

Neutral Earning is money that is made from the Neutral Zone on the Abundance Scale (-1 to +1). It is money earned from a neutral or peaceful feeling place. It is money that you feel neutral about. What are examples of Neutral Earnings from your current life? What made them neutral?

_____
_____
_____
_____
_____

Week 4

Money Love Workshop

Day 2

Abundant Earning is money that is made from the Abundant Zone on the Abundance Scale (+2 to +10). This is money earned from an empowered, passionate, appreciative, enthusiastic, optimistic, happy, loving, or grateful place. What are examples of Abundant Earnings from your current life? What made them abundant?

_____
_____
_____
_____

Week 4

Day 3

Scarcity Earning is money that is made from the Scarcity Zone on the Abundance Scale (-2 to -10). This is money earned from a frustrated, disappointed, worried, resentful, jealous, discouraged, angry, insecure, powerless or fearful place. What are examples of Scarcity Earnings from your current life? What made them scarce?

_____

_____

_____

_____

Week 4

Day 4

Can you ever create true abundance through Scarcity Earning? Why or why not?

_____
_____
_____
_____
_____

Week 4

What emotions do you typically feel on any given day? Are these creating abundance in your life?
Why or why not?

_____

_____

_____

_____

_____

Week 4

Day 6

What emotions do you typically associate with your earnings? How do you feel about the way that you make your money? Is this creating abundance for you? Why or why not?

_____
_____
_____
_____
_____

Week 4

Money Love Workshop

Day 7

What would you think would need to happen in order for you to experience Abundant Earning?

_____
_____
_____
_____
_____
_____

Week 4

Week 5

Recovering from the Truth

Coaching Notes

Date

Money Love Workshop

Day 1

Start an Abundance Journal. This is your work, your practice. Keep track of all Earnings and all Spendings from all accounts including, checking, savings, cash and credit cards each day.

Week 5

ABUNDANCE JOURNAL

Earnings (Cash, Check, Credits, Trade)

Description	$ Amount	Abundance Scale	Type of Earning	Notes about Thoughts and Feelings

Spendings (Cash, Check, Credits, Trade)

Description	$ Amount	Abundance Scale	Type of Spending	Notes about Thoughts and Feelings

Money Love Workshop

Day 2

What have you learned about yourself today?

_____

_____

_____

_____

_____

Week 5

ABUNDANCE JOURNAL

Earnings (Cash, Check, Credits, Trade)

Description	$ Amount	Abundance Scale	Type of Earning	Notes about Thoughts and Feelings

Spendings (Cash, Check, Credits, Trade)

Description	$ Amount	Abundance Scale	Type of Spending	Notes about Thoughts and Feelings

Money Love Workshop

Day 3

Would you do anything different today? Why or why not?

_____

_____

_____

_____

_____

_____

Abundance Journal

Week 5

Earnings (Cash, Check, Credits, Trade)

Description	$ Amount	Abundance Scale	Type of Earning	Notes about Thoughts and Feelings

Spendings (Cash, Check, Credits, Trade)

Description	$ Amount	Abundance Scale	Type of Spending	Notes about Thoughts and Feelings

Money Love Workshop

Day 4

What emotions come up for you while you do this work?

_____

_____

_____

_____

_____

_____

Week 5

ABUNDANCE JOURNAL

Earnings (Cash, Check, Credits, Trade)

Description	$ Amount	Abundance Scale	Type of Earning	Notes about Thoughts and Feelings

Spendings (Cash, Check, Credits, Trade)

Description	$ Amount	Abundance Scale	Type of Spending	Notes about Thoughts and Feelings

www.meadowdevor.com

Money Love Workshop

Day 5

What have you learned about yourself through this process?

_____

_____

_____

_____

_____

Week 5

Abundance Journal

Earnings (Cash, Check, Credits, Trade)

Description	$ Amount	Abundance Scale	Type of Earning	Notes about Thoughts and Feelings

Spendings (Cash, Check, Credits, Trade)

Description	$ Amount	Abundance Scale	Type of Spending	Notes about Thoughts and Feelings

Money Love Workshop

Is keeping this Abundance Journal easy for you? Why or why not?

_____

_____

_____

_____

_____

Week 5

ABUNDANCE JOURNAL

Earnings (Cash, Check, Credits, Trade)

Description	$ Amount	Abundance Scale	Type of Earning	Notes about Thoughts and Feelings

Spendings (Cash, Check, Credits, Trade)

Description	$ Amount	Abundance Scale	Type of Spending	Notes about Thoughts and Feelings

Money Love Workshop

Day 7

How has your relationship to your money, accounts and cash changed this week?

_____

_____

_____

_____

_____

Abundance Journal

Week 5

Earnings (Cash, Check, Credits, Trade)

Description	$ Amount	Abundance Scale	Type of Earning	Notes about Thoughts and Feelings

Spendings (Cash, Check, Credits, Trade)

Description	$ Amount	Abundance Scale	Type of Spending	Notes about Thoughts and Feelings

Week 6

Practicing the Truth

Coaching Notes

Date

Money Love Workshop

Day 1

What differences do you notice in how you think about your money?

_____
_____
_____
_____
_____

Week 6

ABUNDANCE JOURNAL

Earnings (Cash, Check, Credits, Trade)

Description	$ Amount	Abundance Scale	Type of Earning	Notes about Thoughts and Feelings

Spendings (Cash, Check, Credits, Trade)

Description	$ Amount	Abundance Scale	Type of Spending	Notes about Thoughts and Feelings

www.meadowdevor.com

Money Love Workshop

Day 2

How has your story about money changed?

_____

_____

_____

_____

_____

_____

Week 6

Abundance Journal

Earnings (Cash, Check, Credits, Trade)

Description	$ Amount	Abundance Scale	Type of Earning	Notes about Thoughts and Feelings

Spendings (Cash, Check, Credits, Trade)

Description	$ Amount	Abundance Scale	Type of Spending	Notes about Thoughts and Feelings

Day 3

Would you do anything different this week? Why or why not?

_____

_____

_____

_____

_____

Week 6

ABUNDANCE JOURNAL

Earnings (Cash, Check, Credits, Trade)

Description	$ Amount	Abundance Scale	Type of Earning	Notes about Thoughts and Feelings

Spendings (Cash, Check, Credits, Trade)

Description	$ Amount	Abundance Scale	Type of Spending	Notes about Thoughts and Feelings

www.meadowdevor.com

Day 4

Have your emotions changed for you during this process?
Why or why not?

_____

_____

_____

_____

_____

_____

Week 6

ABUNDANCE JOURNAL

Earnings (Cash, Check, Credits, Trade)

Description	$ Amount	Abundance Scale	Type of Earning	Notes about Thoughts and Feelings

Spendings (Cash, Check, Credits, Trade)

Description	$ Amount	Abundance Scale	Type of Spending	Notes about Thoughts and Feelings

www.meadowdevor.com

Money Love Workshop

Day 5

What do you hope to continue as you move forward with your relationship with money?

_____
_____
_____
_____
_____

Week 6

ABUNDANCE JOURNAL

Earnings (Cash, Check, Credits, Trade)

Description	$ Amount	Abundance Scale	Type of Earning	Notes about Thoughts and Feelings

Spendings (Cash, Check, Credits, Trade)

Description	$ Amount	Abundance Scale	Type of Spending	Notes about Thoughts and Feelings

Money Love Workshop

Day 6

One year from today, what relationship do you expect to have with your money, accounts and cash? Why?

_____

_____

_____

_____

_____

Week 6

ABUNDANCE JOURNAL

Earnings (Cash, Check, Credits, Trade)

Description	$ Amount	Abundance Scale	Type of Earning	Notes about Thoughts and Feelings

Spendings (Cash, Check, Credits, Trade)

Description	$ Amount	Abundance Scale	Type of Spending	Notes about Thoughts and Feelings

Money Love Workshop

Over the past 6 weeks, what have you learned about yourself? About your money? About your money-past? And your money-future? How has your relationship to money changed? How has your relationship to yourself changed?

_____

_____

_____

_____

_____

Week 6

Abundance Journal

Earnings (Cash, Check, Credits, Trade)

Description	$ Amount	Abundance Scale	Type of Earning	Notes about Thoughts and Feelings

Spendings (Cash, Check, Credits, Trade)

Description	$ Amount	Abundance Scale	Type of Spending	Notes about Thoughts and Feelings

Made in the USA
Las Vegas, NV
14 November 2021